PLEASE MAKE ME PRETTY,
I DON'T WANT TO DIE

PRINCETON SERIES OF CONTEMPORARY POETS
Susan Stewart, *series editor*

For other titles in the Princeton Series of Contemporary Poets
see the end of this volume.

PLEASE MAKE ME PRETTY, I DON'T WANT TO DIE

Poems

Tawanda Mulalu

PRINCETON UNIVERSITY PRESS
Princeton and Oxford

Published by Princeton University Press
41 William Street, Princeton, New Jersey 08540
6 Oxford Street, Woodstock, Oxfordshire OX20 1TR

press.princeton.edu

Library of Congress Cataloging-in-Publication Data

Names: Mulalu, Tawanda, author.
Title: Please make me pretty, I don't want to die : poems / Tawanda Mulalu.
Description: Princeton : Princeton University Press, [2022] | Series:
    Princeton series of contemporary poets
Identifiers: LCCN 2022000488 (print) | LCCN 2022000489 (ebook) | ISBN
    9780691239033 (paperback) | ISBN 9780691239026 (hardback) | ISBN
    9780691239040 (ebook)
Classification: LCC PS3613.U4225 P54 2022 (print) | LCC PS3613.U4225
    (ebook) | DDC 811/.6—dc23/eng/20220310
LC record available at https://lccn.loc.gov/2022000488
LC ebook record available at https://lccn.loc.gov/2022000489

British Library Cataloging-in-Publication Data is available

Editorial: Anne Savarese and James Collier
Production Editorial: Ellen Foos
Text and Jacket/Cover Design: Pamela L. Schnitter
Production: Erin Suydam
Publicity: Jodi Price and Carmen Jimenez
Copyeditor: Jodi Beder

Jacket/cover image: *Frenzy of Exultations* by Władysław Podkowiński, 1894.
Courtesy of National Museum in Kraków.

This book has been composed in Adobe Garamond

10 9 8 7 6 5 4 3 2 1

FOR LULWAMA

Contents

Let me dance before you,
My love,
Let me show you
The wealth in your house,
Ocol my husband,
Son of the Bull,
Let no one uproot the Pumpkin.

—Okot p'Bitek, Song of Lawino

SUMMER

ARGO, MY ARGO

The mirror's crowfooted
not me. Afro's gone Medusa again.

Every coil's its own Hydra.
I'm adventuring with a comb.

The sink's full of myths . . .
The myths are growing . . .

Every day I find myself
smaller with effort,

my life's light
with every person who

spoke of me. Last night,
Achebe tried again

and I nearly heard him.
Ngũgĩ refuses these tones, says,

this music has the worst sort
of oceans beneath it.

Besides, his ears
are busy with real myths . . .

Being alive must be nice,
says the sink basin, filling

further with myths . . .
I say, *abandon narrative,*

latch onto landlocked
home—forget ships,

take planes! land with
passport onto place

with shore—forget ships,
take planes! land with

passport back to place
without shore—forget ships

for a day sometime on
winter break, during summer—

our only seasons here.
My body's a crowfooted boat

not me. One time I went
blonde, that's a different

prow. One time I went
with suit jacket, that's a different

sail. One time I go
and touch the exact difference,

pretty, sailing, she says, *I love you.*
I say, *whose boat.*

STILL LIFE

Onanism but like coffee without the cream.
My skin yes but also the pointlessness
of our pleasures. In a maple seed's shape
you have copper and plastic inside of you.
Nothing's growing. I don't finish.
So, I'm part of this thing where fish learned to walk.
Your first baby pictures look like seahorses.
We stop now to consider our lungs.
Look at all that we have made
and behold it is very good. Otherwise the pale beginnings
would swim to nowhere, gasping
with gills they do not have
(once, before memory, I made this journey
and found myself
somewhere, slapped
clean and crying with a new soft bottom).
Loneliness. That's one way of seeing it.
A palm wet with dyings.

ARIA

An aria's any song's sympathy with Ophelia
An aria's any darkness
Then any light involved in darkness
Then an aria's like a pool of water
Then an aria's like a painting
Then an aria's like any other sound.

When you're sleeping you sound
And the sound sounds up Karen
And the sound is how I would like to paint
Karen's sounds on my darkness.
The sound is what I would like to be like the mirror
That Karen sinks into her darkness.

Mirrors are little darknesses
Not unlike my mouth how I try sounds
But find water.
I hope someday my mouth finds Karen Carpenter
Even if my mouth is not a mirror it is darkness
Even if the mirror is where her skin eats itself like paintings.

Your skin's not a painting
It doesn't eat itself it doesn't eat my skin's darkness
And in darkness your skin's also darkness.

Your bedsheets make a sound
And the sound sounds up Karen's
Sounds again. You wake and consider me. You pass me a bottle of water

And I drink it. *Then take the bedsheets as water. Then take the air as water*
And now I'm drinking all of you as a painting
—Which is when I hear horses, hear Sylvia:
She's swallowing everything as paintings and her darkness
Is a red eye rising as morning's first sound
Then the horse into that red eye is darkness

Then reading her horse into my black eyes is darkness
Then words are sometimes water
They're the flow of sound
From each to the next, little sips then swallowing then with them we paint
Each other—the darkest darkness
—And I paint you, hear horses, hear you, Ophelia, Karen, Sylvia

Still painting over all of us and the darkness is painting
And the mirror is every little sipping sound in your room's darkness
And the sounds are everywhere like skin like *in this darkness how mine
    is yours*
like any other white girl's, an aria.

MISCEGENATION ELEGY

after Jericho Brown

Let's talk through my window, what it has to do with God.
The stars also suffer. Immense and dead, their gases burn
distant like castanets of antebellum teeth. My open window
a synecdoche of country. No matter how much smoke a pig
roast won't erupt into a song. How its head won't find more
careful music than this apple in my mouth. Pardon his sex,
this apple erupts into violets. Historians archive our care
as an axe upon a ladybird. Air now through my window,
what it has to do with Edith strolling away from me. You
see, I implant now not only a grandmother but a garden in
your tasteless heart. With just that name and its slant rhyme
"Eden," you hear "Gaia." Have you heard a person bloom?
In that garden, Edith's lips hymn. Skyline maintains its mar.
The poem required sound from a body. The poem required
meter heard by those trees. I gift a woman's voice bottled
so cleanly for you. Salt it. And coo admiringly with tongue.
There were other names: *Sogolon, Madhavi, ubume.* Leda.
Ariel. Hierarchy in how I love? Not violets, no—implant
an ending: *known for representing purity, white flowers are
a neutral tone that accents any color.* Camelia. Wisteria. Lust.

CONNECTICUT

Mornings, his wife could not remember who my face was.
Her face stared at me with a mushy smile while Henry ate

the same corn flakes with bananas. I watched the yellow flakes
uncrisping in his bowl of milk, his gums too soft to bear them.

Henry then put me to work on his "fields." I don't know who
first said it. Probably, his teeth cackled "fields" to his friend

who visited him—limping gently—as Henry rolled around in his
red tractor. It roared through his backyard, funneling narrow lanes

into the black, hot soil. Waddling after him in my white sneakers,
I held blue seeds of grass that pricked my fingers. I tossed them

over the soil like a flower girl. "Why are they blue?" I asked him.
"Fertilizer coating," he said. "Dry, mutant rice," said my fizzy mind.

Nights—they opened with heavy sweat—he would sit and watch
Fox News blare. Me next to him, reading a long novel on suffering.

But he shouldn't have paid me as a gardener. I dug about as well
as a child in a sandbox—shallow, amazed by my skinny handling

of that spade. Its crusted rust as dark as my dry skin. No, Henry paid
my hands to hold his loneliness. To hear him. I needed a place to stay.

He liked to hear me singing off-key in the mornings, taking long
cold showers. And walk down these stairs to him: aging, waiting

to plant more blue seeds.

PRAYER

Move *with* me, I said to my brain before it startled itself into a mind. I mind myself becoming this person but without that mind in this world then there *is* no world of me. Then there's old myths of me and they're stuck now inside me. Then sit in churches in my childhood that's where I learn my looking over other people's shoulders. You did not malintend. It happened in that room it did not stay in that room it was as if it were not *with* me. Open that creamy book. Notice now orangutans in all of us, chimpanzees in some of us, gorillas in half of us; and the other half, dolphins. Somehow we all swim. But O I love how dolphins swim, how their blood screams at them when the white moon pulls tides with its myths. . . . And on playgrounds I so badly wanted to *be* a dolphin! Still my fur, how mightily it weighs me as *him*. Were I the son of God and not of my gorilla, would the dolphins still be closest to God. Then the churches still haven't been struck by lightning. Then my country still doesn't have jungles. Or oceans. Where do we come from. I don't know that strange country. Never heard of *her*. Never will.

ELEGY

I have bitten down on the chameleon in my throat. He burst into a single color. Predictably, that lacerated into what white people have since called *sincere* and *quite pained*. And black people continued with their day, never having needed to pretend rainbows to sing. I am flooded with other people's selves, their quiet traumas, their various walking speeds across the river. I have seen someone walk on water. Nor could I blame my father for an event horizon he just happened to have ejaculated me into. Nor could I blame my mother for then having characterized me as ungrateful for the invitation to this . . . party. '90s kids be like, *by the time we showed up all the alcohol was gone.* They drowned. My turn-ons include watching capital explode into non-imagination. Initially: my personal finances, yes, and now: gross domestic products, the ozone layer, democracies. It's been a good season, these few years. Whereas for those without a sense of humor, the idea of skeletons pole-dancing is not appealing. Whereas for those with a sense of humor, the reality of systematic death is also not appealing. Whereas I do not know upon which ground I stand but it looks a little parched. We return to the subject of my throat with the additional question of my ownership: if I pay my taxes, do I belong to myself or do I—you have not attempted to wave away original sin with social contract theory? I mean all genders get along if someone else suffers for peace, says every human arrangement of tar, toil and torture. It's a pretty skyline. In a plane that thunders towards another human arrangement, they stuff me in Economy. There is always someone who works harder than me. There is always someone who is more of a morning person. There is always someone else who isn't as pretty as you.

FILM STUDIES

These black lovers on-screen
save themselves from concrete.

Credits roll. Once, my mother
throws a burnt log at my father,

and it must be like this: holding
on to love's inevitable reel. Once,

the projection streams a finger
corked into a heart: knife-wound.

I tell the doctor, *let go*—unmind
the dark jet when my finger re-

turns to me. Narrative saves us.

If mirrors disappoint, consider
white eyes. Then flood cinemas

with light to drain the mind.
So look at trees neutrally,

says landscapes. A history book
infects them with bodies. I try

a different bingo. I don't go on
walks depending on the news.

There's always news. The lens
should not have considered us,

but there's a block party in the sky.
My ancestors sway. I take pictures

to envy white people. *To envy my-
self*, says mirrors. Shut this door,

walk away from lectures on stars.
Schadenfreude the physicists as

this universe fails us one last time.
The sun's bad season looms calm.

Perhaps we send someone to look,
die bravely to prevent supernova.

My body floats. Earth forgets me.

The producers greenlight a sequel,
watch you finger the burnt popcorn

at the bottom.

POKÉMON BLUE

The virus vacated us. The campus filled with parents' cars.
The plush ones I ordered off Amazon, I left them in my room
fresh and emptied of me, stuffed them into a donation box.

You loved Squirtle most of all. His thin beaky grin—like yours,
mouthing that blue turtle as our child. You held him, pushed him
off your crotch. The cleanest birth ever, you said. But his shell,

there's no way you could birth a shell. Then I said my sister was
sliced out wet from my mother's guts. But Squirtle could swim,
he swam between us while you slept. Our pillow, I watched him

while watching you. Our other children nested on my drawer:
Charmander, flame-tailed lizard; and Bulbasaur, corpse-lily bud.
I met them years ago, thumbs sticky on my sister's Game Boy,

pixels instructing me to choose one to explore a new world with.
I picked Squirtle. Trained him to fight other creatures. Captured
and collected their bodies. Those entire continents of life for me

to catch! Each one with its own theme music . . . I wandered every-
where, listening. Hear music everywhere. Hear the campus yard
sound the largest brass, timpani. Captured from native land, built

by collected slaves. Hear my room swell with shepherd flutes
as if my blackness still sleeps there. Left him. We left them there.
You flew home to California. I sleep in a friend's basement.

Midnight. I wake from a dream where you birth a blue snail.

THE WORLD

This morning this kitchen is problematic.
Every burner on the stove is a capitalist.
I want to sucker punch the Honey Nut
Cheerios but the chapel echoes. Instead
I invent a new pornography: it is soft
embarrassing and difficult. New gestures
are required to teach it. But for myself,
every crucial fingering invites mothballs
from behind a Buddha. What comes first,
moth eggs or the statue inviting them?
You knew, but I swallowed you yesterday
with my palm. Sometimes I hear myself
suckling your toes, making oceans. O
tides, render me gently—desire cannot
make the world. Pure logic says this egg-
soaked bread frying here now is not
a paradox. Because past implies future:
the same egg to crack to soak to fry.
To mother me. And so Darwin purges
toast from his south of France (his anus:
I climb inside it in a dream). More grist
to mill, so Vaseline—hold me gentler
as silicon Epicureans garden on Mars,
quarter tubers on lunar plains . . . Whose
radishes ravish your teeth tonight?
You are too latent inside this spaceship,
exhausts gurgling like open balloons—
and I am air. How you will hear me
whistling while my mind jogs and
orbits Saturn's rings, my palm burning

on my stovetop. The world does not
require you. It is busy and Buddhas you
into bad theories and my heels cannot
cynic for much longer. Plymouth looms
over Pluto. Someone's skin shivers.
But it's quarter to seven before light
reaches out, says, *The question is how
the first molecule arose.* No God accounts
for someone's knowing it takes seven days
before our Earth says, with great feeling,
I just don't want to be with you anymore.

SYMPHONY

Begin as always with a voice.

How long can a frog in a well last?

The well is deep.

(friend, what're you doing down there?)

(friend, when did you start croaking?)

(friend, how high can you jump?)

(jump . . . I could be your princess)

(I'm cute enough to stop you croaking)

(these nights, I also find myself croaking)

I can't jump.

(but . . . I could kiss you?)

(but . . . then you'd kiss me back, green and sloppy)

Please—said to no one in particular—*don't kiss me.*

I went walking in search of the sun after dark.
Like any lover, I'm into failed experiments.
Like any other lover, this is where I succeed best.
I called you. I pissed you off. You went to bed.

So the sun set. I leave bed. I never minded time.
I wanted to break the sun up into amazing bits.
Chew sun-bits as cereal. Make films with that light.
Or rocket ships. Either way: I garden amongst stars.
She thinks I left flowers outside her door. I should
leave flowers outside her door. She wanted me to
leave flowers outside her door. On February 14th,
these flowers I am gifted ready their wilting.
I want you as loud as an orchestra. The quiet is
the loudest orchestra. And people are only always
as large as duos. But I am also something serious
to pay attention to. Should I pay attention, too?
When I do pay attention—I'm sorry. I don't know
when I attend. Maybe—should have been—here.

A croak ascends once more from the depths!

(hey, I think you're kinda cute)

(sorry, I think I should go to bed now)

Going back to bed now. I'm awake too loudly
in the heavy of noon. What's all this speaking
of appropriation? Sounds like violence to me.
Please go away. Please come back. When you
please come back: look a bit more like the girl
with these flowers not gifted from me. Christ,
you *are* a girl with flowers not gifted from me!
Wonder now if any story stands if not on its lone
foot. I called you. You storied yourself again.
I'm sorry for not reading you. Books are so . . .
you know . . . thick. Maybe more so than people,
who at least have the courtesy of talking back.
Okay: say *courtesy*, mean *regret*. I don't have
enough of those, just too many. We are too far
in the evolutionary road of things—thought
is a bit of a curse. I would have preferred touch.
I would have preferred us without the anxiety

of *thought* of touch. I did the mean thing to you.
Another girl does the meaner thing to me. Easy
to not touch only to invoke the thought of *touch*.

(friend, the frog is croaking for us to *touch* it)

(friend, the croaking is a doubling of our lips)

(friend, have I spent too much time with you?)

We only like to kiss girls.

(but I'm not a boy)

Not much of a request.

(not much)

Not much of a demand.

(no, not much)

(you don't have any flowers for me)

The flowers are croaking. The flowers are croaking.

SONG

Forgive myself for breath and I should die.
Self-love an excuse but for that exit: this daydream
of me ended. Of feet parched with weight beyond
the hurt of pale bathroom scale. Or love this
itch between thighs as slower metabolism gifts
slower moods, these dull penetrations of face
into pillowcase. *So die then*, says another country
or lover; splits me long through thoughts of this spine.
And a dream of nerve cells copying beneath this glass.
How inexact to possess skin. Like a flailing sack
too stuffed with consciousness. I feel as a piñata
and you are peckish. Not just the promise of guns shot
but allergic itch draws blood in late summer. I'm sorry
other black men died. I'm sorry I keep thinking,
I look like him. I'm sorry my life feels as easy
as these leaves failing to defend themselves against
their too-soon shifting colors. But I want myself.
I want to want myself as much as I want your shadows
flickering against the walls of this cave, fooling me
of presences beyond myself. And this music: I want this
foolishness of my mouth transmuted into woodwind
and brass. As if this could salve. As if this grass between
my lips epistles this grey sky as any virtue but failed rain.
As if peaches. Forgive myself for breath and this song
should die. I am as new as the paintings in this cave.
Am the same burrowing of grain into body and loss.
Am the same ochre and hematite, inevitable and sorry.

FALL

MY SISTER LIKES GIRLS AND DOES NOT RETURN FOR MY MOTHER'S FIFTIETH

Months after I hadn't had my first oyster
before I came to America. My sister in Canada now

where it starts snowing soon. Things I haven't seen
keep cropping up. Movies are colonialism

and I'm such a dutiful director, swerving cameras
around oceans I hadn't had before. Flying in

I'll ignore the masses of land
locking home. I'll wait for the next flood

to take us once we finish ballooning the sun
and her hot response to our earthly gassiness—

I haven't seen polar bears either yet. My sister
posts pictures of herself

swimming through snow
and the melting goes slow as it can.

Every day I wake waiting for water
as if I'm still home as if my ancestors are still

praying for something as so simple as myself
walking across the river here thinking

when. I'll jump into it in sheer drunken
blaze. My sister had graduated.

My phone's wet. My parents buzz.
The leaves are red

and falling now. Hadn't seen that
before either. I'm always surprised by rain.

SHOWER PRESSURE.
MY BOXES ARRIVE TODAY

so. Everything seems so fragile. Not just this. But press your lips
against this glass of water and break. Its wet surface the glass itself
a slower slip of sand. There are too many ideas. To bear. Wash me
there. I do not bear them they handle me my bedsheets. How much
temptation can a walk hold. No. The river will not end you. Nor
skyscraper at this distance. Nor searing eye of a dog that not seen't
you or look of you before. Or has seen of you. Knows the eyes
of its owners on you after. Please excuse America's first only birth,
it destroys itself. And chooses to. Screams beneath its tarmacs.
Those bones, when my ends kink it falls. Your fingers all over
my heart and skin. *Black*, I continue my long affairs with windows,
the sunlight loves me more. My shadow comes up for air. Against
this projector. No body loves your shadow. The ozone opens a hole
for us. Peer through. Batter me dimly. Patiently. I told you your
future needs a violence my skin breeds. Another continent's walk
is not as this grass. Is not my brother who did not walk. Is not
my father's father, the touch of lightning that seared him in the dry
fields. Don't speak those you don't know. Don't speak of calmlands.
Another tarmac loses you. Unbox it. Say hope.

MASSACHUSETTS

. . . you too, you said with the breath of my lungs. There is only this bed.
Another one of your hairs appears. I am despite decay, whispers this
thinning abdomen. Quietly, a planet's plates shift. A haunched forehead
wrinkling my father's face. And another face behind his neck. I will

grow similarly. Meanwhile, your hair lines here again like another fold
in my bedsheets. Finger it. Pluck. Throw. Another shows. Move on.
Fail to. Relent briefly—and your hairs summon you a little. Disappear
you. Someday, I sweep them off the floorboard. Again not tonight.

Fine then. A glass of water shines there on my desk. Drink this and fill
my throat with dreams. Or space for dreams. Or less cold thirst for
this body to vessel long enough for dreams. To live through rivers. No,
not with these human limbs. But I am a different kind of swimmer,

he says crassly, and wet, hoping your skin will return. Come back. Please,
my throat won't shape stone into life. I labor to cough while your hairs
thin away. And drink another glass. Attempt more breadths of sleep. Dark
wakings minutes before this new sunlight reminds me where. Disappear

you here again. Consider the naming of this place. Who they took it from.
How we once nearly named each other here. November, I am thankful
for the suffering of other nations. How we grasp at solidarity against your
pale kind. I cannot touch your skin. I can only hope for renewal through

erasure of memory. Practice this here. Read another page to. Wake. Drift.
I need you too, I wish your hairs would whisper. Eventually, my ears
will perch towards other imaginations. Even if the only music outside is
the slower injury of crisping leaves. Their patient reds. Time and its

fidelity. Another person
greeting myself.

HALF PAST SEVEN AND

afflicted with such lowness so often no longer sudden

just low

dark sunset small orange left

the sky's a stupid canvas

it's all formless good things have form
that's what skeletons are for

not for cradling falls from towers

certainly not that nor
the crunch of cannibalism

when one bites their nails no

lower then like a mole

I'm digging deeper
like bellybuttons Plato's there

he hates me hate poets I'm banished

lower then so put on
shoes

walk
with each low foot until

sidewalks become mountains

and so the panting follows something real

actually real

real as the thickening
of a child's bones from mash to marrow

to footsteps real

as the fact of it as simple as an apple
does with its sugars real

as going outside being proud, proud of myself for trying,

but where are the apples I thought there'd be apples.

HAMLET TRIES PROZAC

Hamlet tries it and suddenly the firmament's floating.
He takes Ophelia out on a date, says he's sorry for being a dick,
and they make faces at each other over a steak that's too well-done
but he doesn't berate the waiter about it. He just chews the steak
and Ophelia dives into the ribs, stickied fingers playing over
the bones with a newfound sense of comfort. Later, when they take
a bath together, she'll look at his ribs and poke at them, pretend
that in between them flowers might spring out, that imagining
this might make the next bit a bit easier. He's gentle,
which she appreciates, but it doesn't make up for his pale
skinniness. He's sleeping now and she's looking at his ribs, then
presses a finger between two of her own, finds no difference.

HAPPY HAIKU

Lost the will to live?
Dolphins swim further than parks.
Summer won't winter.

*

Then make argument
for various creatures, their breaths
linger in grasses.

*

That I loved once was
clear as carbon monoxide.
Hey, I can't see you—

*

Tomorrow there'll be teeth.
A venus flytrap hickies me.
It's better than porn.

*

—I wouldn't know. I'm
already cicada. Loud,
useless throbs. Like grass.

*

Right ear's still blocked. Spring
flutters to fall. Allergic,
I listen to new leaves.

*

Hold my ribs. There's sky
and it continues. Despite
mind, I live. There's sky.

*

The rain surprises.
And the window surprises.
Now think of the sun—

RENGA (REGARDING
PEOPLE WHO FEEL
SORRY FOR ME

WITH THEIR WORDS
"BEYOND WORDS" WHICH
"NO WORDS CAN EXPRESS"

HOW "WITHOUT WORDS"
THEY FEEL WHEN SOMEONE
WHO LOOKS LIKE ME DIES

WHILE OPENING HIS THROAT
WHILE I SAY "PEOPLE"
BUT MEAN "YOU")

Yes. I did love that
aquarium, loved how its
mercy reflected

in my *blank* child's stare
into the endangered pod.
Yes, said I'm *black* so

the orcas gained minds:
eventually they walked
onto shore. Don't *shoot*.

Language did not fail us:
we *shot* them all on the shore,
then learned to swim.

FILM STUDIES II

I don't hate it here. Nor my need to be illuminated.
Or to find myself in a museum, cautiously advertised
in a pamphlet. The statues fall at noon. We pull them
to the sea. Midnight I dive to press myself against bronze.
How I enact white guilt: patina. Fine. I hate it here, just a little.
Let's meet like parallel lines. Or where you cut your finger
while you snip film with that special knife. The source
of the word *cut*—cut past the resolving image of your scar—
cut past my breath. Leave reels. In the prequel I am given
a backstory. Critics adore me there. Holding gold
at the ceremony, I mouth appreciations. I say *O*. Maudlin
tongue, they stream me away. Someone as black as me
drowns. I sip red wine. The image recedes. The water echoes.
I hate that voice. I hear it here. It lives there in my teeth.

NOVEMBER ELEGY

It is not cold enough. For my tastes,
I'd like it even warmer. But there's
the fact of this going Earth, speaking
against its changes by showing us
what it once was: a confused tree buds
earlier than it should. The sun returned
shortly for one week. It was easy to be
alive. For just then. Even if everything
was suffering. My loss is as any. Some
one I will say I once loved. You did not
die. After this Earth, I could not have
known that it will be easier to pretend
you as deceased. Privilege speaks back:
those bodies back home. I don't listen.

PRAYER

Everything I like is like that man who first thought to take that picture of that starving black child waited for by that black vulture in that Sudan. I like what I write. I am hurting myself by liking things. My words are maybe taking pictures of myself starving me. I tell myself stories in order to clutch my throat. My throat is clutched. Please make me pretty, I don't want to die. I want to sleep now. I know I am holding this so tightly with sleep. I know I am screaming towards this with my sleeping. People are not asking of us because they are busy. I am not asking of us because I am simulating being busy. What should we ask of in a world whose only word is *work*? This is the best deal. This is the unasked-for gift. If I saw a starving black child my first thought would not be to take this picture of myself. Or wake. Everyone is dying. There are such pretty words for this.

MY BROTHER DOES NOT RETURN
FOR MY MOTHER'S FIFTIETH

Egg that could but did not quite, I see you in their
museums, the coal-dark African masks, your blank

face. To not find you walking with me with these
stolen faces, to not find you crawling up from dust—

I left you landlocked with our parents, heard tides
before my body, wet axes carving shore to noise,

and who has ever rescued the drive home? Washed
my crusted hands and what—stubborn grains. Dried

my hands with a cold towel, your little hands dried
but could not hold their shores—though other grains

now live between your fingers. This world will not
hold little hands but turned to dust. At this party,

I sip on bitter-dark drink, bearing warm speeches
while your body turns to airlessness. My thoughts

on this glass, roundedness of your once new skull
I never saw. My flight returns to their shores. Your

face escapes me.

NEAR IT

Please no longer the need to be harmed by colors.

The streets in this continent change as easy as fingernails
latching onto me when you breathe like this. Press hard.
Your skin bruises easy as leaves. I watch leaves cold now
while lonely cars glide past the playground. No matter this
light that flees early, I allow myself this. I amass a nest of
smaller rays—the birds do their final gathering and I am

gone again, returning for the rest of this day. Here,

an old tree. An old tree by this fence. An old tree by this fence
by this road. Gravel intermingles above soil with newer reds
revealing themselves as leaving. To beneath roots. Shall I press
myself against brick? Pretend? Yes: that I *was* here, *will* hear
beneath feet beneath brick beneath leaves above you, will hear
all along the mass of days in which another dry conflagration

falls into this box of tissues and sanitizer. Leaves, then
my kids' hands, finally quiet in the classroom. Masks. I clean
their hands and think again of their minds, stumbling across
mathematics. Imagine the soft marvel of another planet
where other minds do not stumble, cannot marvel, cannot *I*
but only sing. One song and I am the last thought on Earth,

the fantasy of Schubert's four hands, I am not dying.
I am not immediately dying. Or I do not *know* that I will.
For the backache, the doctors scan my heart and find my right
ventricle might be thicker than it should be; the left ventricle
pumps oxygenated blood to the body. I am so close to safety
I could confirm it now: in my chest, a dream gone, breathing.

WINTER

ALL WE GOT WAS AUTUMN.
ALL WE GOT WAS WINTER.

nothing was fervent. nothing was budding. everything was
the sickness and then my bed. everything was all midnight all
touching myself in dark corners hoping for release. constantly
finding myself awake in mornings despite the persistence
of retreating. how to sleep forever without dying. how to sleep for-
ever without depression. how to sleep forever but someone notices
long enough to come and wake you into spring. then summer.
then everything I wanted was the birds bothering me with all
their muchness outside my window. everything was love, love
my season and still the mother sicked herself to sleep with gas
and she did not wake up. I remember her every day and pretend
a love of both poppies and horses and bread and milk. how I miss
her. watch from the ashes and no one rises and how men continue
to breathe this air. almost thankful for not being consumed
but to instead consume. almost thankful for my bones if not for
the fact of my back. depended on you. you depended on nothing
but pictures. would wish myself to end if not for the fact my love
for the birds and the bees. wished myself into tears. somewhere else
an ocean roars I do not see it I do not hear it, I brush my teeth.

SATURDAY MORNING MY HAIR
MEETS THIS DRAIN

The blinds I fold open to
so many sunflowers would sing—
outside, a girl is image-making.
Fall into her: be American.

And see that girl fall into ground.
Her eyes sing wetly, the wet joins snow.
Her gloved hands rub her red face red.
Leave my window—her parents' eyes.

Shower, scrub hard:
no American girl pressed beneath.
These kinks clog beneath.

NEARNESS

Make me as nail and finger
then cross of nails through
hands with fingers.
That's not the love I want,
I say to my feet who walk
on water with storm around
me. My friends watch from
the boat. I watch my friends
from the boat. Their toes
are clammy. Notice her toes
are clammy when I visit
an other and the other takes
me with the hush of want
some boy wished for as his
mother slept. Some girl now
wishing with her own voice
I hear only years from then.
Now hearing what I hadn't:
clavicles, sternum, coccyx.
Soon I'll hear crow's feet.
From the church book water
storms from the priest's mouth
with the hope we'll hear it too.
I hear children jumping into
puddles. Hoping they're mine.
Hoping their clammy toes
make some other nearness.

FORGIVENESS ROCK RECORD

& where should I find myself if not in my mother's eyes or my father's
     hands or my sister's care
for the world. & if I should die I should die because that is the way
     the world was designed. & what was
the thing that drew me up from myself as if a river flowed upwards
     towards the pull of the moon. &

would you not want to be a tide-song, called for constantly by the
     mere fact of rock: large, white, above:
asking you to be real by virtue of movement, of its heaviness regarding
     movement & to be seen as a slow
tragedy of the sun's shadow.

I am asking for this life to call for me. I am asking myself to call for
                                        the acceptance of this skin, its pre-
dispositions, navigated keenly by eyes which aren't my own. by histo-
     ries pieced and un-pieced together
by various arguments of *human*, sometimes even of *love*—like watch-
     ing those that were born before me

decide they were this *thing* called *human* & summoned themselves.
     What is there beneath the rock is it
as heavy as the rock itself. American cartoons said that the moon was
     made of stinky cheese. I thought

marshmallows. Or of another sweet I cannot recall that bursts into
     powders of soft sugar upon biting it. Or
maybe it is the cautious marble of a jawbreaker (so large that my sister
     and I stored them in the fridge &

licked them over the curve of days leading up to some other sort of
     awareness. Somewhere along the line
she is wronged: touched. It might have been then. I couldn't see.
     Didn't see. She's older. I was greedy &
eventually its big sphere would soften to a pearl, its wrapping finally
     larger than the thing it held). Maybe

dear moon, what I am asking of you is to become this sun, or vice
     versa, or why can't I sleep for as long

as I used to. It is not that I don't want to be alive (he says
     convincingly) but that there is a calmness of

constant possibility that sleeping affords, that to be woken so early, so
     constantly now by my body as if

he is begging me, really begging me, to *change my life* to not reach the
     age of *I have wasted my life* to say
to itself that *I have a life* to say to others *I want to be in this world* to
     really be able to hear the words

*I love you & I want to be with you & you're a good person & people like
     you & you're beautiful &*

not want to instantly retreat to some question of how unlike the moon
     is to the sun, but how they hold

one another, even if one is nearly always disappearing. Yes, that's what
     I wanted to hear: myself
as if I were another person in another's mouth. As if that were what it
     is to live. Okay. So maybe it was.

ELEGY

from weather. Everything this morning is white and light is low. I played adult on the playground, watched them. Now their sodden soles, melting into the classroom's linoleum. I want to preserve their bodies in warmed amber. They will quiet then. Then I might lift them into the next springing of clouds with sky not just white, not just constant frothing of white speck and flash of white reflected, returned to this hemisphere: to when I was as small as them. To say *as a bud* is too much. But nearly once, when with the growing of cells into mass then weight then me, I was *as a bud—budding*, evinced by the hardening colors of a skid knee, the closeness of blood unto memory and how long until I forget my mother. She also breathes. I could apparate her here, silence her how I could not otherwise. Or gesture her kindly, like weather. See. She dances now for no body watching. She pirouettes inside a phone call I ignore while the denseness of the real appears through the windows. They named it *snow*. Simple prettiness, I call your whiteness to hold us less barren each year. *Would you stop screeching your desk on the floor?* My mouth to a child.

SECOND SONNET

is about you: not your father who mildly streams you
down your years. I pretend a knowing of your skin or
beneath it the wells of yourself over the time it took
you here. Where and who do I go with without
myself? The long widths of you across a year of
myself near you—shuddered now by another mind—
I am in need of me. You pan your lens towards
another version of your old man. You have constructed him. I hear
an aria again, I want to think *strawberries*,
I think *mulch*. There is too much potential in this dying
planet not to believe you are at the end of this. Yes even I
hear you long enough to hear another person: and think she
was as clever as you said you were at the start of this: who
is not the point. I meant this Earth.

THIRD SONNET

is not about you. I am capable
of drafting these winds in my chest. Ease my mouth into
even newer music. I am as a crow in
a basket of French fries: sudden slow the drip
of me inside you. There was another set of persons
who might have otherwise obliterated a small nation
but instead insisted on a walk, considered
a dog—and moved on. The statue I'm eyeing
in this country would have wanted me dead or
at the very least deeply unhappy. This is not another race poem
but often I look at us and cosplay radicalism.
Can I lie to you quickly? I have never wanted another
version of events. This is my best life. All my life
is with you even on Tuesday.

FILM STUDIES III

I don't watch myself, others
watch then draw. You draw
me with your lens—it asks
where my skin is bred, films
my right eye, its oddity: white
dot in pupil. Where a doctor
saw no harm, my mother eyed
its lonely milk. See me gently
inside while your lens seeks
my "white thoughts," hidden
inside my pupil's black. My
thoughts, I thought, were color-
less. Or I thought you thought
this. Or hoped this. Or what is
your lens' draw of me. You
said you'd ask of the white dot.
And you ask of everything but
the white dot, the white dot's
draw of everything else of my
skin—always this soft excuse
for everyone to ask me of every-
thing but me. My skin is every-
thing, is everything and me,
anything but me, is me—but
you *ask*. It does not belong to
you, I can't make it belong to
you—and my girl makes films.
I write. Everyone must draw.
She is sometimes white. She is
sometimes not. And I am black,

I am sometimes not anything
but black. Is drawing like breath.
Breathe gaps between my lips.
Breathe gaps between my teeth.
My girl makes films. My girl is
not my girl. I am not my girl's
boy, not your boy, and what is
being drawn if not who. And
who is anyone to draw but love.
Your lens here, my girl, my love—
is what you ask with it—of me—
of you of me—is it black. It is
nothing. It is almost me, almost
black. Coax it. And it breathes.
Touch me. And it breathes back.

NEWNESS

Make me clean and pretty as
a blade of grass called upon
a mouth to sound a whistle.
Some things I can't do. Find
time for myself with my hands.
Find time for myself with other
hands. Every hand's a whistle
says my oral fixation in near-
aria, looking for an ear as well
as a carpenter's skill to smooth
my wood's surface. Inside any
wood's the memory of termites
even if you aren't here in me
says my imagination in near-
choir, looking for more ears as
pebbles called across water by
a child's hand. My mouth in you
a stone boat. I'm flying now
I think—really—as any mind
showers themselves into new
skin every morning. Troubled
my mornings with dreams. I'm
warring with alarms looking for
treaties against entropy. Snooze
most standoffs for ten minutes
at a time. Then the gushing of
electrons fizzing themselves in-
to awareness of themselves. For
not having jumped yesterday off

a really tall building in search of
the final snooze. I'm nearly here
since my hair's towel-dry wet with
dreams of someone so unlike you.

PRAYER

Though I fail you generously and deeply, I fail you vertebrae, arpeggioed rosetta, I fail you ribs, glockenspieled rosetta; I carry your stone down with butterfingers and how early your shuddering mountain. . . . Mist, blue sheet-music, sciatica. The long nerve stretches into aching fibers: it does not gift my black mother white wings. The Earth looms again Wagnerian-heavy and American cows stumble onto it with thick warm gasses, readied now to be minced through drive-thrus. Sweetly, you press tar onto soil. I examine pictures of us. My coccyx is gemstone. It waits for your eyes to fill it with light. Where I pressed my lips to you, flower me there. Nearly every gender humors me with silence. Nights I wish your thin nails come dancing. Nights I wish my legs look keener than purity. My mottled thing I love you, my rattled thing I love you. My embryonic curses, I muzzle you here as rose-tinted lens. I promised you. They cannot see us here. Please. Fail me harder fail me faster *yes*, fail me.

FRENZY

after Sylvia Plath and Władysław Podkowiński

Hey horse, hey friend,

I like chrysalises. We need more tenderness,
not less. Emerging from a foreign field,

my neck in your arms. Pale arms, holding a black-berried set
of eyes, holding me. I loved you,

loved you further than the recesses of myself into
my melanin. Hey horse,

stagger me downwards with a blacker blackness.
Event horizon me. Pupil me. Flat-and-sharp-key

me. Eyelid me before the opening of

an aubade. To die pretty as lace: these poppies
re-engineered for an imagination beneath my

shirt. I skirt around this handling of my body
of me, tonguing so sweetly, my hair. I curl for you with a largesse

unheard of by my ancestors. And I cannot resent
the woman I love. The woman I love

will touch my hair. My hair will

touch myself when the light spills open,
fresh as the disaster of lungs. To speak with the certainty of

your fingers pulling out my tongue. The snow outside
and the shadows of ourselves against the walls—

nothing here is racial. Only our usual pleasure
igniting itself into another pale exultation of

unborn children. Divine me. It will only make me feel
more real to know the pain of your mind,

thinking somewhere, riding into another red sun
not imagined by me. Still, the indefatigable hooves beat

only for every other woman who has loved me, beat
only for you as I have made you here. And another horse

on this horizon, holding me as myself, inking itself
into dawn. I am alive. Pretty.

NOT A SNOW DAY

Please stop. Enough froth over this land
and the traffic fills with impatient radio—

or radio's the only pinprick of voice
nearer now than skin. A child asks to touch me

and I tell her not to. She pokes me.
I swab the itchy lengths of my nostrils and God

says again, *do you like it when I touch you*
like this? Everything familiar and awful always

and the test tube carries me to a lab. This morning,
the shower's water is careful and warm. But the air—

I walked in late to school and the same child here
waiting just outside the door, sleepy and shivering.

I sanitized her hands. I teach her how to divide.

SPRING

GOOD LONG POEM

was something I always wanted. Because something was never working
    inside of me.
Because something is never working inside of me. I'm working now,
    Sabrina, at the writing
the way that you might be working, but not as well, not as frequent,
    not with the casual
viciousness of your words. was something I always want. Because of
    my attraction to plants,
I'd like to be buried in soil, be buried soft, be buried deep (I want to
    take a nap again, I always
want to take a nap again), with only the minimal awareness of things
    such that the sun is
something I might turn to, slowly. I'm a little bit vampiric. I'm into
    mouths. I'm into necks.
I'm into singing things. I'm heavy with all sorts of muddled horns.
    Long, hollow, cold.
Spittles flying all warm and solid. I'm aching with it. Please let me
    ache with the warmth.
Please ache with the warmth with me. was something I will always
    want. Please let me want it
with warmth. Every day's feeling like a shipwreck. I'm moored to the
    land in a hopeless way
with kind, unnecessary energy. A shallow well, my mind's a shallow
    well. Bad echoes
of other mouths. Also muddled horns. All the muddled horns. With
    one girl: a flute. I miss her.
Here. I'm listening to the air now and there is no history in it. I'm a
    builder of large things
like the wind. was something I want. I'm building a new version of
    history that involves us

with the wind. I was walking and nearly got carried away. Air can be
  thick. I'm wading now
in the gas. Lungs are thick. All the cognition is being the chest rising,
  hold, then falling.
All the cognition is something I want, always. Even the plants, mouth-
  less, are opening
something like lips to their thinking. Turning now to the sun. There's
  snow. Turning still
to the sun. Here. Working not the way that you might be working.
  Because something will
never work inside of me. Placing it here with warmth, with need. Wet
  air. Then brass.

AFTERPARTY

Brahms rang in again, or the clarinet rang
in again, or the violins thread in through
the door. So my cochleae itch in grass
in spring, the widening of throat and gums
to pollen, smaller than sparks of closed
eyelids, ringing still after staring down
the sun. I wish our world's end as peaceful
so possible. That we might have okay sex
all the time. That we might each sing this
song we must sing, so everything rings
as this grass did my mouth. But I don't
ask to be so reminded of you. Nor do I
know you, ever. You say riding a bicycle
might whiten me enough to keep me
safe. I frisk for you while stores burn
for murdered black people. I didn't need
to know you to know me. You rode me,
I wished you more. You sang often. Listen:
to bring my own mouth to myself might
summon the home I was raised in for you—
and my mother and father, my sister, my
brother. Strangle me instead with threads
of other lungs now. Let the German play
in place of my mouth. Let this rain settle
for the clear sky over my dry home—my
mother, father, my sister and brother, you
heard of them in the sunny park in the big
American city we watched films in. Friends
call from elsewhere. They sound of semen.
Your hands over my mornings. They call

from everywhere and they will sound your
plain red mark on my bedsheets. From that
time. We were all friends, the same sheets.
I left them, then swallowed the birds' beaks
the next evening.

EAR

Van Gogh's ear is lying now without Zyrtec in a field
abstracted here into this concerto for a single voice.

Forgive then this invocation again to paint my face,
but I feel necessary when my tongue is in your cochlea,

wherever it is imagined: certainly not in a memory of
the phone call when I last heard her say my name . . .

So turn stars into milkshakes! Your hands were unsteady:
genius or syphilis? Everything is feeling. Every dead brush-

stroke a reason to outlive yourself here with me in this
field and hear syllables gallop as bright as sunflowers,

not the quiet pink roses I gifted her. Everything is
feeling. When you frame me like this I am capable

of posing for a kind of humanizing that none can hard *r*
or bar or batter or break up with. Everything is with you,

always with *you* Vincent, since no other ear can so co-
inhabit my lungs, nor can feel—*with* me, *with* me—

the devastation of our audience. A quiet phone. A memory
as bashful as wilted pink roses on a countertop. Nowadays,

I cook alone. My hands steady with garlic, cloved with
a warmth only its crushing can bear—

VERTEBRAE

More of you. The choice between water and mud
and mud turning into water anyway. Things wash themselves
is what the clouds kept saying. The stream shallows
then breaks open with new wash months later then goes again
into startled coda. Like sleep. Found another stone
and it was not filled with secrets. All it wanted to say is
that it's been here a long time. And that when it was larger
an even longer time then. I did not hold it it was too heavy
to even touch. In the corner of this a child throws it across
the stream and there starts something else entirely known.
When you said to me that there's something in my teeth.
You called it a smile. I sound it out again and again.

PRAYER

for lost causes like the gravity of granola in mornings. The heaviness of missing bacon fat. Or the folds of you when you stretched on top of me then back then forth. Or the calling of us in the long day times and the reappearances of birds like mixtape summers. It sounds the same. And the need for dancing with our toes stumbling on pebbles as cold waltz. Step in and the showerhead forgets its place, decides where to make of your shadow, where to kill its flickers. Step out and a mouth belts out cries for other mouths having been there. Answer for this via what it wants to order in the restaurant. In the yellow fields outside, the crickets sound our irritations. Some sweaters age faster than skin, the itch a reminder of dry riverbeds. Walking across homelands after the longest time, those winters, this spring. The core of a star as kidney stone. The heat, the salt it thaws. Let our insides become as the grips of polar bears after our breaths. How I've seen this. This seeing feels new.

ELEGY

My life tomorrow, will it sleep. I don't know if other dances are with me. Not only that I've just cut my toenails, but that frightening impotence of my pillow during the day. . . . When I asked for the beloved, did your voice sound as a torn leaf. Pressed you to my lips and not even the faintness of a whistle. Pretend symbiosis, your skin. Its inner resources revealing myelin. Iai unsheathed. Hey, love—to be so gorgeous is sin. So declares my facial hair while withering its patchy borders. If I said I loved you, would the bicycle not abandon itself into a line without a pedaler. Invoke again the transcendent sky. It turns the copper sulfate color of an experiment during a life-defining exam. Breathe with me. So, brain decides it wants to be with myself. So, all you have is your voice, I. If another brain complains of another unnamed *thou*: then *fugue*, let everything be fugue. All heartbreak is the exasperation of collective unconsciousness. Movies exist. When you stopped singing, I heard the clouds darken. To remember you properly, say, a face, limbs, a glimmering neck, or teeth bedazzling as ancient sewer pipes. . . . Here then, name this impulse towards your death, *my* lungs. That they shrink then enlarge. Nothing is as threatening as a pattern. Nothing is as precise as the casual nuisance of a neuron deciding light. Dare me to say your name and see the lightning brighten softly. I tire of the burning bush. I tire of the well unlit by the technicolored dream coat. Also of the quiet theatre, regretting psalms. Carefully. Scratch this screen. Dial the code and get lucky. My voice begetting song. Begetting not brain, but mind. Sing with me, love. What music is left is the calm disappearance of ice from poles, the smiling of children before the end of children. Listen: a love song is complete with discord. You call it *life*. I say *respiration*.

POEM ABOUT MY LIFE MATTERING

after June Jordan

Asked myself this morning—this usual—where is black life
found? Surely not in an atlas given how they cull the size
of the Continent down as carefully managed roach control,
But other nights I hear myself singing down a well and it sounds
a trumpet or at least the mouth of Joseph trying to have a good time,
you know? When the stars decided the fly tanning on Mike Pence's
picket-fence hair—was that black life? And should I shed myself
of that chitin and decide *this* black self—and so *grow a spine*—
who must I show it to? I wouldn't recommend history either,
But black life died for me to sip high-fructose liquids with less ice:
no matter whose skin I wear I can't laugh at that. A parallel history
is right next door and the neighbor's dog keeps barking my name.

ARIA

O half moon—

Half-brain, luminosity—
Negro, masked like a white . . .

    —Sylvia Plath, "Thalidomide"

There is not enough light inside this poem to
Lie to you. All my poems are in whiteface. Which makes me clean,
    bearable. Is my life viable. This poem

Is not mine. Every morning I carry it
More than this strain in my jaw. When I recite you my memory does
    not recite me back. I call out for you

And my mother answers *please call*
Us back. I am compared to my father. A moth falls from my lamp.
    Choked by light, by glass. Choke me

Harder. There is pleasure inside
This horizon, bending. These legs sleeping in my bed, they vessel me.
    Peel him. I taste of lobster beneath.

You peer at me. I am peerless. The best
Of my skin you will witness. I am all bodies like this body—yours to
    take only if you will have me dark

Enough. As a horse's eyes, like berries I
Rot black in your throat. And I am so pretty with the chance of my
    blood in the air, these clouds suffused

With a warmth unseen until police draw real guns at me. Remember
    the boy with a name with a toy gun
In the park. Their imagination kills him.

My mouth is a real gun. My ears warm in
Your tongue. It, too, sang America. Poem, stay with me. Float with
    me. This white page peels a black boy

In a park. There is no light inside him.

AFTER HISTORY

Has anyone managed to make a world.
After race we turn to genetics, return
after to the archives for new history. Who
then determines when we're from. Roots,
we learn to speak of them. The baobabs do
not speak of themselves. We hear wind flee
through their leaves. We see our minds feast
through bark as ants warring with termites.
Has anyone managed to make themselves.
We wonder our excitement when we see
only our wide teeth speak, only our large lips,
anything so small as proof that we could not
hold one another. We do maybe. We did not.

AMERICAN ELEGY

I know no music for how a country should end.
I no longer want to be pretty for you. Not even for
myself. If I must watch you burn while performing
my own arias, then I will watch you burn with my
throat. If I must sing another world to live, then my
tongue arrives earlier than the final star in this brief
stretch of time called a self. In the classroom today,
another child practices purring. On all fours, she
crawls up to me and presses her hair and ears against
my leg: and it is the truest thing to happen to my skin.
I move back to scold her. She laughs. And I laugh
with need. I needed you, America. I needed to speak
another world into my lungs. This piercing instrument
of my clavicles stretched towards sunrise—they sing
for you my throat phlegming from tar to tongue, sing
for you my lips brushing yours, burning and black.

POETRY IN AMERICA

Green, firm, your father prods at the stems above with a fruit picker pole. Mangoes. From Florida. Mailed from Massachusetts to Nebraska. Large letters name me, name you. Open the battered box, think *Egypt*. And the purple petals you mail from Massachusetts to Vermont. Wipe down flight seats with wet-wipes, sudden air. From Vermont. Hear you here now in Nebraska, where spring gutters in the back of my throat. Where my nose leaks. Where my right ear refuses air. Hear you from the hospital where you call in Massachusetts. Let my left hand hold your throat through my phone. Hear your brain swallow you. *Be sure to put them in a brown bag to ripen.* I watch the faucet spill at night—the slightest turn—my fingers gummy with orange flesh and orange threads of flesh. You snap yourself in mask, before air. To Florida. My phone streams you. You prod at the stems above with a fruit picker pole. And what is it? Too many birds, none of you. See the hazy look of you with white sterile background before they take your phone from you. Wait for *Unknown Number* to light up during the day while scrolling through remains of eyelids burst by rubber bullets, bitter clouds of tear gas passing through crowds, police cars roaring towards bodies. Listen to my friend's neighbor cough bulbs of mucus into his kitchen sink. And while walking past his backyard, stare once by accident through the glass door. See it. The purest white flowing from his throat. Hear you ask again when I can see you. In Massachusetts. Say my luggage just arrived from Vermont. Wonder where you get your phone. Wait for your friends to tell me what your doctors say. Reflect on synapses. Imagine yours stirring while you said just two days before the sterile white—how America is watching you. Realize that America is. Remember you with your hijab. Remember your hair instead. Laugh with you about mangoes, this century's season of diasporic karaoke, classics from the ancestors, the lyrics read *please be with me*. I don't want to sing anymore, now read *I don't want to be alone*. In Nebraska. Place more orange flesh in my mouth when my friend's mother again asks me to eat. Taste how the sun glows from Florida, think *Egypt*. And what is it? Dvořák, String Quartet No. 12: *I am convinced that the future music of this country must be founded on what are called Negro melodies.* I say this land does not belong to anyone. I let my hair kink in shapes. I try love myself in the mirror. I conjure you next to me before closing my eyes. Listen. The waves. The screaming beneath them. It carries over to you. Walk with me there. The shore. The ships. And then name what it is: Alabama. Alaska. American Samoa. California. Connecticut. Delaware. Florida. Georgia. Guam. Guantanamo Bay. Hawaii. Louisiana. Maine. Maryland. Massachusetts. Mississippi. New Hampshire. New Jersey. New York. North Carolina. Northern Mariana Islands. Oregon. Puerto Rico. Rhode Island. South Carolina. Texas. United States Minor Outlying Islands. United States Virgin Islands. Virginia. Washington. Philando Castile's daughter, *it's okay Mommy.* Philando Castile's daughter, *it's okay I'm right here witchu.* Philando Castile's daughter, *Mommy please stop saying cusses 'cause I don't want you to get shooted.* Philando Castile's daughter, *I can keep you safe.*

CLARITY

is difficult. Resist it. To illustrate:

I was riding my bike and got hit by a car.

Was it a sunny day or a cloudy day
and which do you like best?

It was a cloudy day. I ran the red light.

No angel appeared about a knife in my hand
meant to end a small life.

Only a physics I plainly miscalculated.
And my eyes opened

seconds later with my body lying on the road.

So it will continue, I thought.

This plainer knowing that this life
is not my life. Is not my parents' life.

Is only the plainest organization of molecules
made into my feelings

about suns or clouds and thinking

endlessly which you might like best
and not knowing how to actually ask you.

*

Let me tell you this instead:

I saw Mahid riding his bike yesterday.

I was walking towards the school
I spent nine months with. It was really him,

his happiness—his body skinny and black
and riding so fast with a smile that could cure

a heart. Let me tell you this:

I hate how much I needed his heart

on another cloudy day.
That I walked towards the school

after I cleaned my room
and found a note amongst my dry sea of invoices.

That little note he wrote me

knowing that I'm moving soon to New York
to sit at a desk to make rich people richer

and maybe siphon money away from places
like the Continent that I was born in and

that Mahid's parents were born in and—

Dear Tawanda wakanda forever

by by I won't see you again
hope you go to Magazen Pool so I can see you again.

So I walked to Magazine Pool,
and felt stupid standing there.

So I walked to the school playground,
and his bike appeared.

*

All music is meant to be resisted anyway.
It isn't natural

to bring a mouth to an ear like this
(again)

to need so urgently to tell you this
(again)

as Wordsworth embodying children
like some eager tapeworm:

Our birth is but a sleep and a forgetting . . .
I love that poem

with the same distance that I love Mahid.
Every day and with the distance

of someone with a mouth

deciding that if no one hears them,
they might die.

But he recognized me

while on his bike
from the black brace on my left wrist—

cracked numb from when I met the car.

His smile was wider than my room's windows.
I think I want to live

too often sometimes
because the terrible sound of this world

can reduce itself to a smile.

I hate admitting this to you.

That there is nothing less complicated
than loneliness.

That I cannot hear you
with your own voice.

That to be clear is to resist, with great difficulty,
your own ears.

Acknowledgments

A selection of these poems appears as a chapbook titled *Nearness*, published by *The New Delta Review*. Many thanks to their editorial team, especially Ian Lockaby, for believing in my work. Thanks also to Brandon Shimoda, for selecting my chapbook to be published: I owe you the world.

Endless thanks to the editors and readers of the following publications, where many of these poems first appeared or are forthcoming, often in slightly different versions from here:

Afternoon Visitor, "Vertebrae" and "Good Long Poem"
The Baffler, "Frenzy" and "American Elegy"
Black Warrior Review, "Clarity"
Brittle Paper, "After History"
The Denver Quarterly, "Elegy" ("I have bitten down . . .")
The Florida Review, "Renga"
Gigantic Sequins, "Afterparty"
The Harvard Advocate, "Argo, My Argo" (also republished on *Mass Poetry*'s website)
Hobart, "Still Life"
Hobart After Dark, "Happy Haiku"
Hoxie Gorge Review, "Nearness" and "Half past seven and"
Lana Turner, "Aria" ("An aria's any song's sympathy . . ."), "Aria" ("There is not enough light . . ."), and "Poetry in America"
The Massachusetts Review, "all we got was autumn. all we got was winter."
The New Delta Review, "Film Studies," "Prayer" ("Though I fail you . . .") and "Film Studies II"
The New England Review, "Connecticut," "Song," and "My Brother Does Not Return for My Mother's Fiftieth"
The Night Heron Barks, "Near It"
Off the Coast, "Third Sonnet"
Palette Poetry, "Miscegenation Elegy"
The Paris Review, "Second Sonnet"
Perhappened, "Forgiveness Rock Record"

Peripheries, "Elegy" ("My life tomorrow, will it sleep . . .")

Pigeon Pages, "Pokémon Blue"

Post Road, "Massachusetts"

Postscript, "Prayer" ("Everything I like is like that man . . .") (also reprinted in *Peripheries*), "Hamlet Tries Prozac," "Saturday morning my hair meets this drain," and "Not a snow day"

A Public Space, "My Sister Likes Girls and Does Not Return for My Mother's Fiftieth"

Rejection Letters, "Poem about My Life Mattering"

The Rutherford Red Wheelbarrow, "November Elegy"

Salamander, "Prayer" ("for lost causes")

Salt Hill Journal, "Newness" (also republished on *Verse Daily's* website)

Tupelo Quarterly, "The World," "Symphony," "Elegy" ("from weather."), "Film Studies III," and "Ear"

Lastly, the epigraph for this book as a whole is excerpted from *Song of Lawino*, by Okot p'Bitek, courtesy of East African Educational Publishers Limited. Copyright © 1966, 1967 by Okot p'Bitek. The epigraphs of the two 'Aria' poems are excerpts of "Ariel" and "Thalidomide" from *Collected Poems* by Sylvia Plath, courtesy of HarperCollins Publishers and Faber and Faber Limited. Copyright © 1960 by Ted Hughes.

*

Thank you to Susan Stewart for selecting this manuscript for publication, and for the kindness of your phone call during a difficult time.

Thank you to Anne Savarese, James Collier, Ellen Foos, Jodi Beder, Jodi Price, Carmen Jimenez, Bob Bettendorf, Pamela L. Schnitter and everyone else at Princeton University Press for making these strange words into a (touchable!) book.

Thank you to my teachers: Michael Patrick Allen, Lisa Ampleman, Robert Balun, Josh Bell, Ana Božičević, Jennifer Chang, Heather Cole, Henri Cole, Teju Cole, Bojana Coulibaly, Christina Davis, Jay Deshpande, Kelebogile Ditsele, Camille Dungy, Andrea Eaton, Mercy Erbynn, Bernard Ferguson, Darcy Frey, Catherine and Robert Ganung, Jorie Graham, Mary Walker Graham, Alistair Haggar, Emilie Hardman, Robert Hass, Brenda Hillman, Ken Hincker, Abdul Hoosain, Major Jackson, Jonah Johnson, Loma Jones, Jamaica Kincaid, Katlego Kai Kolanyane-Kesupile, Mark

Levine, Ada Limón, Jesse McCarthy, Campbell McGrath, Morwadi Moilwa, Gomolemo Motsamai, Maria Muller, Annah and Clayton Ndlovu, Virginia Parker, Tefo Paya, Victoria Queneau, Vidyan Ravinthiran, Peter Sacks, Vijay Seshadri, Will Shotwell, Jonathan Tafila, Andrew Taylor, Peter Vernon, Alan Wilson, Matthew Zapruder and so many more—

(But thanks especially to Josh and Jorie and Jay, who read and reread this endlessly in its earlier drafts. Josh, for his warm prodding. Jorie, for her patient commitment to form. Jay, for his narrative touches.)

Thank you to all who I was with when we were writing with Josh and Jorie and Jay and . . .

Thank you to Tin House Books, Brooklyn Poets, the New York State Summer Writers Institute, and the Community of Writers for support towards writing this book.

Thank you, Cal Bedient, Clifton Gachagua, and Tracy K. Smith for your kind and thoughtful words endorsing these poems.

Thank you to the students and teachers at the Morse School in Cambridge, Massachusetts. I miss you all unbearably.

Thank you, Alex, for goats. Thank you, Amrit, for rollercoasters. Thank you, Bianca, for scratchy sketches. Thank you, Carissa, for flowers and edits. Thank you, Charlie, for chancing the chapbook. Thank you, Darius, for elegies and emails. Thank you, Disha, for marvels. Thank you, Edith, for lyric and tenderness. Thank you, Egshiglen, for goofiness. Thank you, Emma, for prose and the J-Man. Thank you, Haolun, for reiatsu and tweets. Thank you, Harry, for paws and seashells. Thank you, Isabel, for song and bawdy phone calls. Thank you, Ivy, for cats and squiggly handwriting. Thank you, Jade, for winter gummies. Thank you Jithya, for geeky pixels. Thank you JMC, for being offline with me. Thank you, Johnny, for those morning walks. Thank you, Khanyi, for soft large laughter. Thank you, LG, for touch. Thank you, Marcelo Hanta-Davis and family, for the beats. Thank you, Marie, for earnestness. Thank you, Mohammed, for every playground jutsu. Thank you, Muhua, for long-distance films. Thank you, Neil Band and family, for making me less skinny. Thank you, Rishi, for spellcasting. Thank you, Rufaro, for dead guitars and IPAs. Thank you, Sabrina, for magic and crispiness. Thank you, Salma, for you. Thank you Sasasa, for the vibes and heart. Thank you, Selah, for always dancing. Thank you, Sherah, for Lacan and Zoom. Thank you, Siyanda, ke a go rata. Thank you, Spencer, for steak and *Contra*. Thank you, Sofia, for chrysalises and hugs. Thank you Tiff, for looking. Thank you Tjawangwa, for paving a way. Thank you, Vamika, for every year, every country.

Mama and Deddy, I'll be home sometime. Lulwama and Azha, I love you.

Aabilwe, take care, wherever you are.

Thank you to everyone I've missed, and you.

Notes

"Miscegenation Elegy" borrows the phrase "*known for representing purity, white flowers are / a neutral tone that accents any color*" from an article titled "40 Types of White Flowers" on the Florists' Transworld Delivery website's blog. This poem is written after Jericho Brown's "The Tradition."

"The World" borrows the phrase "*The question is how / the first molecule arose*" from Jostein Gaarder's novel *Sophie's World*, translated by Paulette Møller. The phrase "The world does not / require you" is borrowed from the title of the Rion Amilcar Scott short story collection, *The World Doesn't Require You*.

"Prayer" ("Everything I like is like that man. . .") references Kevin Carter's photo *The vulture and the little girl.*

"all we got was autumn. all we got was winter." borrows the phrase "love, love / my season" from "The Couriers" by Sylvia Plath. The phrase "watch from the ashes and no one rises and how men continue / to breathe this air" is a spin of the last stanza of "Lady Lazarus," also by Plath ("Out of the ash / I rise with my red hair / And I eat men like air.").

"Forgiveness Rock Record" takes its title from *The Broken Social Scene* album of the same name. The phrases "change my life" and "I have wasted my life" are riffs off the last lines of Rainer Maria Rilke's "Archaic Torso of Apollo" (translated by Stephen Mitchell) and James Wright's "Lying in a Hammock at William Duffy's Farm in Pine Island, Minnesota" respectively. That whole "life" sequence of lines is inspired by Terrance Haye's "American Sonnet for My Past and Future Assassin" ("Rilke ends his sonnet, "Archaic Torso of Apollo' saying. . .").

"Frenzy" borrows the phrase "indefatigable hooves" from Sylvia Plath's poem "Words."

"Poem about My Life Mattering" is written after June Jordan's "Poem about My Rights."

"Poetry in America" takes its title from the television and college course series of the same name, created by Professor Elisa New, who teaches at Harvard University. The quote from Czech composer Antonín Dvořák is attributed to an interview he did with *The New York Herald* in 1893 during his years in America. The italicized speech near the end of the poem is transcribed directly from publicly released dashcam footage of the police car holding Philando Castille's daughter and her mother during his shooting by officer Jeronimo Yanez on July 6th, 2016, in Falcon Heights, Minnesota.

CPSIA information can be obtained
at www.ICGtesting.com
Printed in the USA
JSHW010553061022
31328JS00005B/7